THE BEST BOOK OF

Ancient Greece

Belinda Weber

KINGFISHER

BOSTON

Contents

KINGFISHER

a Houghton Mifflin Company imprint
222 Berkeley Street
Boston, Massachusetts 02116
www.houghtonmifflinbooks.com

Author: Belinda Weber
Publishing manager: Melissa Fairley
Art director: Mike Davis
Consultant: Dr. Thorsten Opper,
The British Museum, London, England

Main illustrations by Chris Molan

First published in 2005

10 9 8 7 6 5 4 3 2
SBC/0405/WKT/SGCH(SGCH)/128KMA/C

Copyright © Kingfisher
Publications Plc 2005

LIBRARY OF CONGRESS CATALOGING-IN-PUBLICATION DATA
has been applied for.

ISBN 0-7534-5871-3
ISBN 978-07534-5871-6

Printed in China

The early Greeks

The first people to live in Greece —almost 40,000 years ago— were Stone Age hunter-gatherers. They moved from place to place in search of food. As people learned to farm the land they grew crops and stayed in the same place. Small groups of people could live together happily, without worrying about finding food. Early civilizations developed on the Cyclades Islands in the Aegean Sea. The Minoans settled on the island of Crete.

Early writing

Many Minoans could read and write. They turned the picture writing of ancient Egypt into a style of handwriting, which was called "Linear A."

Living the high life

Minoans were farmers who grew crops such as wheat, barley, olives, and grapes. They also raised sheep, goats, and cattle for meat and milk. They built huge palaces—the finest of which was at Knossos.

The Palace of Knossos

The Minoans decorated the walls of this palace in Crete with beautiful paintings. They often painted the creatures they could see from the island such as dolphins and fish.

Aegean
Sea

Greece

Cyclades
islands

Early Greek
settlements

Crete

The Mycenaeans

At around the same time as the Minoans were living in Crete, another civilization developed on the mainland. The Mycenaeans were warriors, and they were ruled by kings. They traded farm produce and pottery for gold and ivory. Mycenaean craftsmen were very skillful and made many beautiful objects, including fine pottery and gold ornaments.

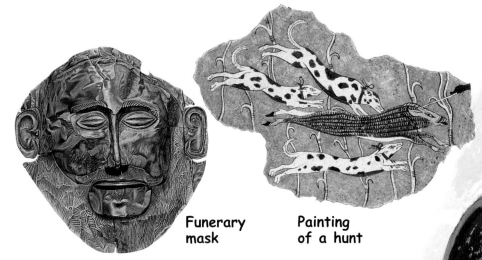

Funerary
mask

Painting
of a hunt

Fine craftsmanship

With a settled society, not everyone had to farm the land in order to produce enough food to eat. Some people developed other skills. Craftsmen used local clay to make decorated plates and goblets. They then traded these items for gold from which to make fine funerary masks. These masks were used in royal burials.

6

Strong walls

The Mycenaeans built their city on top of a hill so that they could see any attackers as they approached. The city had strong walls made from huge blocks of stone, and the gate was decorated with two lions. No one knows why, but the city was abandoned or destroyed by around 1100 B.C.

The tale of Troy

When Mycenae's major cities were destroyed, Greece entered the Dark Age. People did not learn to read, but instead they listened to poets telling the great stories from the past. One poet named Homer told how Helen, the wife of the king of Sparta, was kidnapped and taken to Troy. The tale explained how the Greeks tricked the Trojans into letting them into their city.

Heinrich Schliemann studied the ruins of Troy.

The Trojan horse

The Greeks made a large wooden horse, which they left outside Troy's city walls. The Trojans were curious and dragged it inside. That night soldiers hidden inside the horse crept out and opened the city gates, letting the Greek army in to destroy the city.

Finding out

German archaeologist Heinrich Schliemann discovered that Troy was on the Mediterranean coast of modern-day Turkey. His research found not just one city there but many, all built on top of each other.

Settling new lands

No one knows exactly what happened during the Dark Ages. We think that people no longer learned to read or write, and that is why they did not keep written records. As populations grew, there was not enough food for everyone. Trading posts were set up, and Greeks started to settle new lands. They moved around the Mediterranean coasts—to Italy, Sicily, Africa, France, and Spain. With easy access to the sea, the new settlements began to trade wine, olive oil, and honey for grain and timber.

Settlers arriving at a new colony

Trade

The Greeks were successful farmers and traded their surplus crops for other items. Greek craftsmen used the new materials to make bracelets and pottery.

New colonies

Many of the new colonies were set up around the Mediterranean and Black Sea coasts. These places had good natural harbors and plenty of land for farming.

France

Spain

Italy

Sicily   Greece

Africa

■ Early Greek colonies

Building new homes

The new colonies built temples and houses for the new community.

 The Greeks who stayed behind formed "city-states," which were made up of the city and the surrounding countryside. The largest was Athens, which was rich and powerful as it had its own silver mines and a port. After the expulsion of the last tyrannical ruler, Athens was run by its citizens—men who were born in the city and could cast votes to determine how their city was run. It was the first democracy, where citizens made decisions.

Athena

Athens was named after Athena, the goddess of wisdom and warfare. The Greeks built the Parthenon, which contained a huge statue of Athena, because they believed that she protected the city.

Having a say

City-states had their own governments and ways of doing things. Meetings were held around 40 times a year, and all citizens could vote.

Greek citizens had the chance to question other people's political views during debates.

People inside the Parthenon

Sparta

Sparta was another important city-state. It was ruled by two kings and had a council that made all the decisions—they were very strict and demanded obedience from their people. All Spartans, both men and women, had to be physically fit and trained in warfare. Spartan soldiers were the strongest in Greece.

Training hard

Life was tough in Sparta. Only the fittest babies were allowed to live—officials decided which newborn babies would survive. Boys left home at the age of seven to be raised with other boys. They trained hard and became soldiers.

The man behind the idea

Lycurgus was the ancient Greek statesman who set up the military city-state of Sparta. Lycurgus showed that military training and physical fitness gave the Spartans an advantage when fighting against other city-states.

The oracle at Delphi was said to have foretold the laws of Sparta. Her priest read the laws to Lycurgus.

Girl power

Spartan girls were also expected to be physically fit so that they could produce healthy babies. They were encouraged to compete in sports.

15

Great ideas

Ancient Greece was the home of many great ideas. Meetings were held often at which any citizen was allowed to speak. A well-presented argument could change the way that people voted, which meant that education was also important. Boys were taught to read, write, and make speeches.

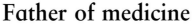

The Greeks brought offerings to the god Asclepius with the hope that he would heal them.

Understanding math

The great mathematician, Archimedes, was in his bathtub when he solved a mathematical problem. He shouted out "Eureka!," which means "I've got it!".

Father of medicine

The ancient Greeks understood how the body worked and were able to treat many ailments. They also prayed to Asclepius, the god of medicine. The Greeks offered pictures or carvings of their wounded limbs with the hope that Asclepius would cure them, and many believed that sleeping in his temples would improve their health.

Political life

Citizens' meetings were held outside the city walls on a hill called the Pnyx, which was close to the Acropolis. An Assembly was the most important type of meeting. There voters decided on political issues.

Daily life

In ancient Greece most married couples lived in households that were made up of their elderly parents, children, and slaves. Men born in the city-state were called citizens and had the right to vote. Women, foreigners, and slaves did not have this right, and they had to follow the decisions made by the man of their household. Very few women held powerful positions in society.

Storeroom

Greek streets were often smelly and dirty, with open drains. Most houses faced away from the street.

Toys and games

Greek children did not have very long to enjoy their childhood. By the time they were 15 years old many boys were training for the army, while most girls were married. There were no schools, but boys from wealthy families were taught by private tutors. However, Greek children still found time for toys, including dolls and toy horses.

18

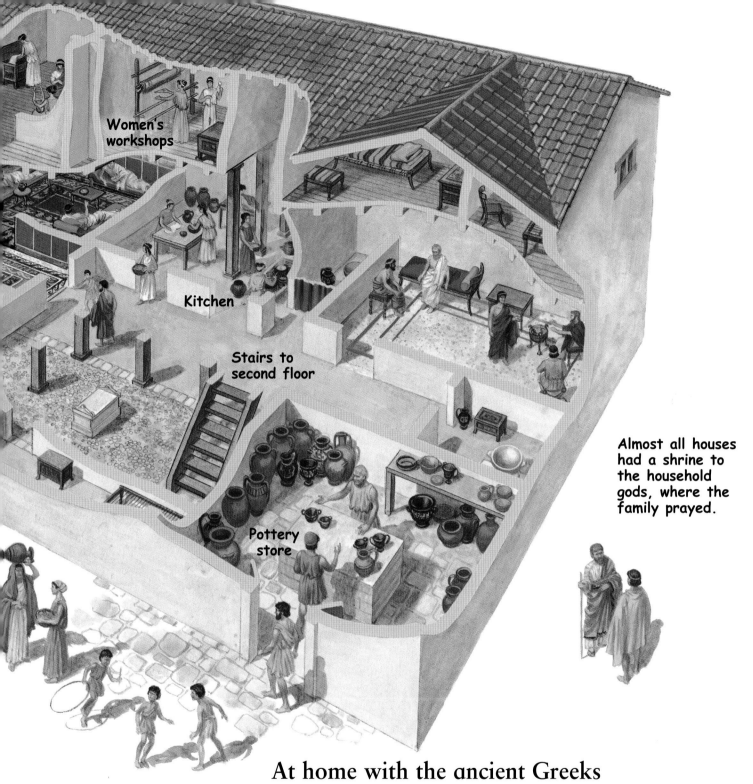

Women's workshops

Kitchen

Stairs to second floor

Pottery store

Almost all houses had a shrine to the household gods, where the family prayed.

At home with the ancient Greeks

Many family houses were built around an open courtyard, with the rooms opening onto it. This house is also a potter's workshop and store. The family lived at the back, with their bedrooms and the women's workshops upstairs. Any slaves would also have lived upstairs.

Festivals and games

The Greeks always found time for theater, music, and dancing. Physical fitness was highly prized, and the Olympic Games were held in honor of the god Zeus. Like other sports competitions, the Olympic Games were open to all Greek city-states, and there was fierce rivalry. Champions were crowned with olive leaves.

Good sports

If city-states were at war with each other when the Olympic Games were held, a truce was called so that everyone could take part in the games. Winning athletes were treated like heroes.

Many of the sports in the Olympic Games are still played today. Throwing the javelin is one of them.

The theater

The Greeks loved going to the theater. All the parts were played by men, who wore masks or brightly colored clothes to distinguish their characters.

Winning the Olympics

Winners were rewarded with crowns of olive leaves and had ribbons tied to their arms. They were given free food for life in their home city-state.

Racing separately

Girls were not allowed to take part in the same competitions as the boys were—they had their own races.

21

Armies and war

Sparta was the
only city-state with
a full-time, fully trained army.
In other city-states all citizens were
part-time soldiers, who were expected to drop
everything and help fight during times of war.
Most wars only lasted a few
weeks, and survivors were
soon back home again.

Eyes and faces
were occasionally
painted on to the
ships to make
them look more
frightening.

Foot soldiers

Greek foot soldiers
were called hoplites and
were a very important part
of the army. Many Greek
battles were fought with lines of
hoplites marching up to the enemy
and hacking their way through.

Fighting at sea

Many Greek battles were fought at sea. Special warships called triremes were used. Teams of 170 oarsmen rowed the ships, powering them along at high speeds. The ships had a huge battering ram at the front to crash into enemy ships and cause maximum damage.

Fighting on horses

Soldiers had to buy their own armor and horses, so only the wealthy soldiers could afford to ride. They formed the cavalry, and they could charge into enemy lines, making gaps for the hoplites.

23

Gods and goddesses

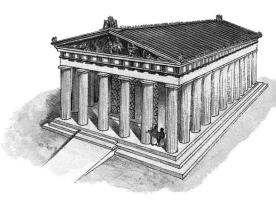

The ancient Greeks believed that gods and goddesses controlled every aspect of nature and had power over their lives. Each city or town had a guardian god or goddess to look after them, and temples were built in their honor. Ceremonies were also held to ask for their protection.

Temples

Ornate temples were built to please the gods. People prayed to the gods to help them with their lives.

Generous Greeks

The Greeks offered sacrifices to their gods. These could be animals—usually sheep—or wine or oil. Each offering showed that the Greeks were generous to the gods.

Gods at war

Even the gods fought wars and battles. In one myth Zeus led the Olympian gods against the Titans—the Titan leader, Kronos, was Zeus' father.

Myths and legends

The ancient Greeks thought that their gods lived as one large family beyond the clouds over **Mount Olympus.** Their gods looked like humans and had many of the same qualities and faults—they even argued and disagreed with each other. The Greeks celebrated their gods with stories and legends telling of great acts of courage and bravery. These stories helped them understand the world in which they lived.

Flying horses

Pegasus was a winged horse that carried the hero Bellerophon into battle. But when he tried to ride into Heaven, the gods got angry. Pegasus was stung by an insect and threw Bellerophon off his back.

One-eyed monsters

Cyclops was a storm god who made thunderbolts for Zeus. Legend tells of how the hero Odysseus defeated Cyclops in one of his many adventures.

Into the labyrinth

When Theseus set out to kill the Minotaur that lived in a maze called the labyrinth, he unwound a ball of string as he walked. After killing the monster he found his way back safely by following the string.

How do we know?

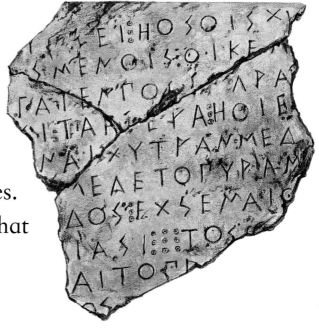

Wealthy Europeans started collecting statues and pottery from ancient Greece in the A.D. 1700s. Archaeologists studied buildings in order to learn more about the history of the places. They also found pottery and works of art that helped them understand how people lived.

Temple carvings

Many temple walls were decorated with carvings. They tell us how important the gods were to the people and how they worshipped.

Written records

Many inscriptions were carved in stone. These help us understand more about daily life for the ancient Greeks.

Digging up history

At an excavation a lot of care is taken not to damage any of the remains. The soil is sifted through to make sure that nothing is missed, and every find is checked carefully.

Greece today

Many of the temples and buildings that are mentioned in this book can still be seen today.
Greek cities, such as Athens, bustle with life and are popular places for tourists to visit. The mixture of ancient and new combines a sense of history with the enjoyment of a modern lifestyle.

The Parthenon

Originally built as a temple, the Parthenon is still an inspiring place to visit. It is made of stone and marble and has beautifully detailed carvings in the panels.

Tourists visiting the Parthenon

Glossary

ailment A minor illness or disease.

ceremony A ritual, or formal act, performed to mark a special occasion.

city-state A Greek city and its surroundings that had its own government.

colonies New settlements set up away from the mainland but often paid for by the Greeks.

courtyard An outside area within the walls of the house, which is open to the sky.

craftsmanship Skill at making works of art.

Dark Age A time period that little is known about.

democracy A system of government in which citizens can vote on issues. Citizens usually elect representatives.

funerary masks Decorative masks that are placed on the faces of dead people before they are buried. They usually look like the person.

guardian Someone who takes care of someone else.

Minotaur A mythical creature that was half man and half bull.

oracle A spirit who could tell the future or give wise advice—often speaking through priestesses.

ornate Beautifully decorated.

shrine An altar or place to worship a god.

survivors Those who stay alive or unhurt in spite of an event such as a battle.

thunderbolts Powerful blasts of thunder that were used by the gods.

trading posts Places where surplus goods and foods could be sold or traded for other goods.

truce An agreement to stop fighting.

tyrannical Describes an absolute ruler who has taken power by force.

Index